My New Book of Words 1

Nina Gontar

Queensland

Name: _____

My New Book of Words 1: Queensland

Text: Nina Gontar
Illustrations: Nina Gontar
Editor: Jarrah Moore
Designer: Karen Mayo
Production controller: Renee Cusmano
Reprint: Siew Han Ong

Acknowledgements
Dedicated to my son Justin, with thanks for the happy memories and hopes for a successful future.

ISBN 978 0 17 019523 2

Cengage Learning Australia
Level 7, 80 Dorcas Street
South Melbourne, Victoria Australia 3205
Phone: 1300 790 853

Cengage Learning New Zealand
Unit 4B Rosedale Office Park
331 Rosedale Road, Albany, North Shore NZ 0632
Phone: 0800 449 725

For learning solutions, visit **cengage.com.au**

Printed in Australia by Ligare Pty Limited
2 3 4 5 6 7 18 17 16 15

Contents

The Alphabet

apple — *a*

balloons — *b*

cat — *c*

dog — *d*

egg — *e*

fish — *f*

girl — *g*

horse — *h*

igloo — *i*

jam — *j*

kite — *k*

lamb — *l*

mushrooms — *m*

needle — *n*

owl — *o*

pig — *p*

queen — *q*

rabbit — *r*

snail — *s*

tent — *t*

umbrella — *u*

vegetables — *v*

whale — *w*

X-ray — *x*

yoyo — *y*

zip — *z*

Rhyming Words

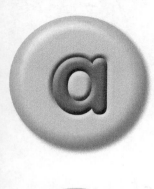

bad	cat	back	all	bang
dad	fat	pack	fall	hang
had	hat	track	hall	rang

bed	bet	men	deck	bell
fed	get	pen	neck	fell
led	let	ten	peck	sell

big	bin	lick	bill	bring
dig	fin	pick	fill	sing
fig	tin	sick	hill	thing

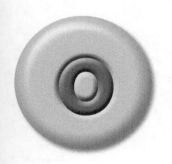

dog	cop	block	dolly	gong
fog	drop	clock	holly	long
hog	hop	lock	jolly	song

but	bun	cub	buck	flung
cut	fun	grub	duck	hung
hut	sun	rub	luck	lung

ants

apple

April
August
Australia

about   all   as
add   am   ask
after   and   at
age   any   aunt

New Words

Rhyming Words for

bad
glad
had
sad

My **dad** gets up early.

_____

_____

_____

bag
gag
sag
tag

These are my **flags**.

_____

_____

_____

back
lack
pack
stack

I have a **black sack**.

_____

_____

_____

bang
gang
hang
rang

I **sang** this song.

_____

_____

_____

"ai" or "ay"?

I can play in the rain.

New Words	

again	paint
aid	rain
bait	stain
chain	train
main	vain
paid	wait

_____ _____

_____ _____

_____ _____

_____ _____

_____ _____

_____ _____

New Words	

away	play
day	ray
gay	say
holiday	stay
lay	today
pay	way

_____ _____

_____ _____

_____ _____

_____ _____

_____ _____

_____ _____

b

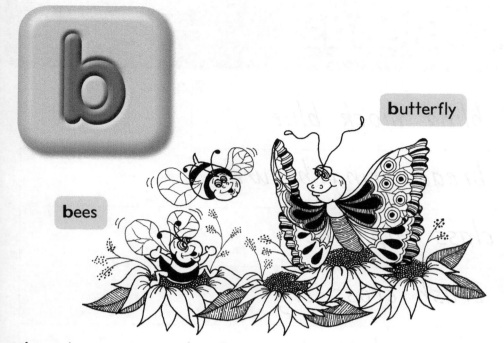

bees

butterfly

B

Ben
Benita
Brisbane

back	before	birthday
bag	behind	book
be	between	boy
because	big	by

New Words

9

Blends

bl	black blast blind block blue	
br	brag brain bread bring brown	
cl	clam clap class clip clock	
cr	crab crack crash cross cry	
dr	drag draw dress drip drop	
fl	flag flat flip flop fly	
fr	free fresh friend frog from	
gl	glad glass glove glow glue	
gr	grab grand green grin grip	
pl	plan play please plug plus	
pr	press pretty prince print prowl	
sl	slam sleep slid slip slow	
sm	small smart smell smile smoke	
st	stand step sting stop story	

C — cat

C — cow

Canberra
Christmas
Christopher

cake   car   come
call   clap   could
came   climb   cry
can   colour   cup

New Words

When "c" and "h" stand next to each other ...

ch is their new sound.

champ	check	chips
chance	chest	choke
chat	chill	choose
cheat	chin	chop

chickens

_____ _____

_____ _____

_____ _____

_____ _____

_____ _____

watch

arch	peach	_____
beach	pinch	_____
bench	reach	_____
ditch	rich	_____
fetch	search	_____
French	teach	_____
March	teacher	_____

Words Ending in "ck"

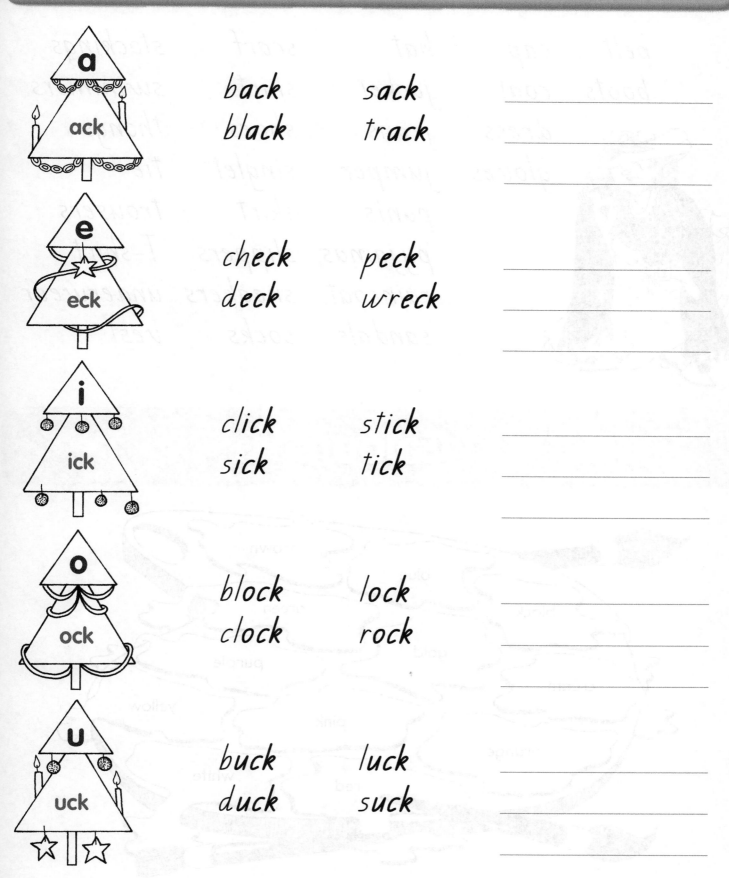

a — ack

back   sack
black   track

e — eck

check   peck
deck   wreck

i — ick

click   stick
sick   tick

o — ock

block   lock
clock   rock

U — uck

buck   luck
duck   suck

Clothes

belt   cap   hat   scarf   stockings

boots   coat   jacket shirt   swimmers

dress   jeans   shoes   thongs

gloves jumper singlet   tie

pants   skirt   trousers

pyjamas slippers T-shirt

raincoat sneakers underwear

sandals socks   vest

Colours

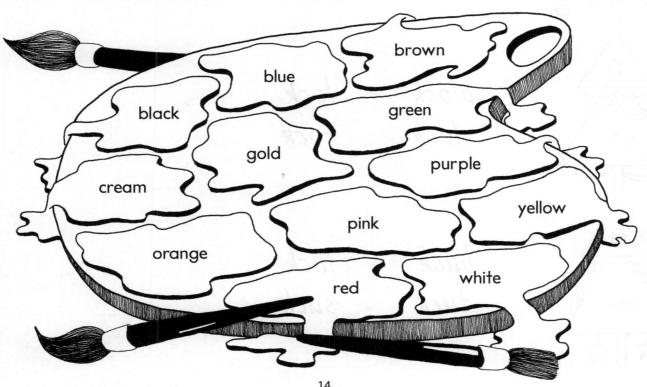

brown

blue

black

green

gold

cream

purple

pink

yellow

orange

red

white

Contractions

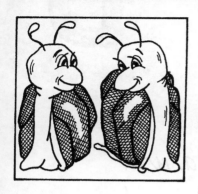

Join two words together.

Make one new word called a contraction.

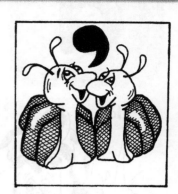

I am an apostrophe!

I am written to show you where the missing letters were.

There I am!

I'm taking the place of the letter **a** in **am**.

I + am = I'm

My list of contractions

are + not = aren't

can + not = can't

did + not = didn't

have + not = haven't

I + had = I'd

is + not = isn't

that + is = that's

was + not = wasn't

you + are = you're

_____

_____

_____

_____

_____

_____

_____

_____

d **D**

dog

dinosaur

Darwin
December
DVD

dance	do	dozen
day	does	draw
dear	dollar	drop
dig	down	dry

New Words

Adding "ed"

bang	help	limp	pick	
banged	helped	limped	picked	
bark	hope	mend	play	
barked	hoped	mended	played	
call	jump	park	thank	
called	jumped	parked	thanked	

Double the last letter before you add the new ending.

bat	hop	rob	tip	
batted	hopped	robbed	tipped	
drop	nod	stop	trip	
dropped	nodded	stopped	tripped	
grab	pop	tap	whip	
grabbed	popped	tapped	whipped	

e

E

echidna

elephant

Easter
Ellen
Eric

each	egg	everybody	
ear	elbow	everyone	
easy	empty	everywhere	
eat	every	eye	

New Words

Rhyming Words for

fed
led
red
sled

This is my **bed**.

_____
_____
_____
_____

jet
met
net
pet

This duck is **wet**.

_____
_____
_____
_____

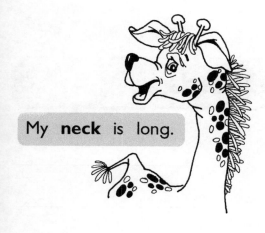

check
deck
peck
wreck

My **neck** is long.

_____
_____
_____

bell
shell
tell
well

I **fell** over.

_____
_____
_____
_____

"ea" or "ee"?

I can see the sea.

ea		New Words
beat	leap	
cheat	meal	
deal	meat	
eat	neat	
heat	real	
heater	seat	

ee		New Words
bee	keep	
deep	queen	
feel	reed	
feet	seed	
heel	seen	
keen	week	

f F

frogs

fish

Fatima
February
Friday

_____
_____
_____
_____

family   few   for
fast   first   friend
father   fly   from
fell   football   funny

New Words

Family Photograph

parents

man
father
dad

woman
mother
mum

relatives

uncle
aunty

children

boy
son
brother
teenager

baby
child
infant

girl
daughter
sister
kid

grandparents

grandmother
grandma
nanna

grandfather
grandpa
poppy

cousins

niece
nephew

grandchildren

grandson
granddaughter

Feelings

I feel
angry.

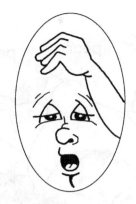

I feel
embarrassed.

I feel
excited.

I feel
happy.

I feel
mean.

I feel
proud.

I feel
scared.

I feel
surprised.

I feel
upset.

Fruit

pineapple
grapes
banana
apricots
watermelon

pear
peach
oranges
lemons
strawberries
apples

cherries

Farm

barn
bull
calf
cattle dog
cow
crops
donkey
duck
duckling
farmer

fences
field
foal
goat
goose
guinea pig
harvester
hen
horse
lamb

paddock
pig
pony
ram
rooster
shed
sheep
tractor
truck
water tank

g G

goat

girl

Gavin
Germany
Gina

game	glue	good
gave	go	grab
give	goes	great
glass	gone	grow

New Words

Garden

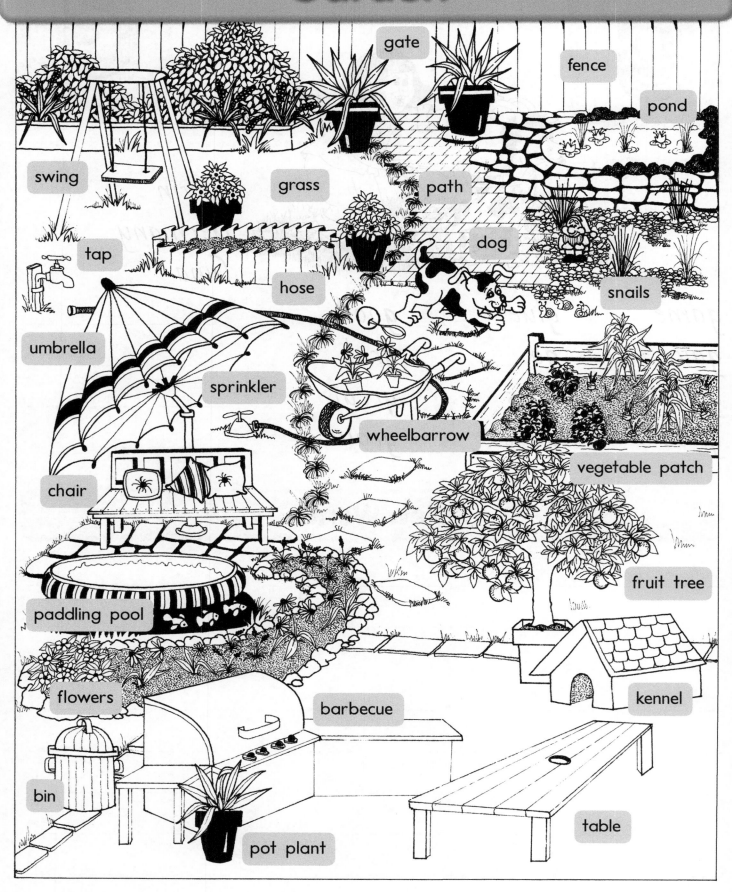

gate

fence

pond

swing

grass

path

tap

dog

hose

snails

umbrella

sprinkler

wheelbarrow

vegetable patch

chair

fruit tree

paddling pool

flowers

kennel

bin

barbecue

table

pot plant

h   H

horse

half

Halloween
Hanukkah
Hobart

had	help	his
has	her	hit
have	here	home
he	him	how

New Words

Hobbies

exercise

fishing

football

gardening

gymnastics

horseriding

knitting

music

painting

reading

sailing

skiing

snorkelling

soccer

surfing

swimming

insects

ice-cream

I'll
I'm
I've

idea   inside   it

if   into   itchy

ill   is   it's

in   isn't   itself

New Words

Rhyming Words for

Sit!

bit
fit
hit
lit

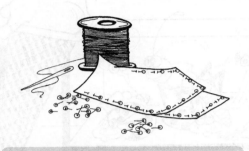

bin
din
fin
win

Pins and needles are **thin**.

_____

_____

_____

I'm **sick**!

flick
kick
lick
pick

I stand **still**.

bill
fill
hill
will

_____

_____

_____

Adding "ing"

bark	catch	fish
barking	catching	fishing
help	jump	keep
helping	jumping	keeping

The cow needs **milking**.

Drop the silent "e" before you add the new ending.

give	hate	love
giving	hating	loving
make	race	take
making	racing	taking

Dancing is fun.

j

J

jars

juggler

January
July
June

jacket   job   jug
jam   join   jump
jeans   joke   jumper
jet   joy   just

New Words

koala

kangaroo

Kara
Khai
Kokoda Track

		Silent "k"	
keep	*kill*	*knew*	*Kara*
kept	*kind*	*knife*	
key	*kiss*	*knock*	
kick	*kitten*	*know*	

New Words

l

L

lion

lemons

lamb	leg	long
last	like	look
lay	listen	lost
learn	little	love

Lan
Liz
London

_____
_____
_____
_____

New Words

_____ _____ _____
_____ _____ _____
_____ _____ _____
_____ _____ _____
_____ _____ _____
_____ _____ _____
_____ _____ _____

Words with "ll"

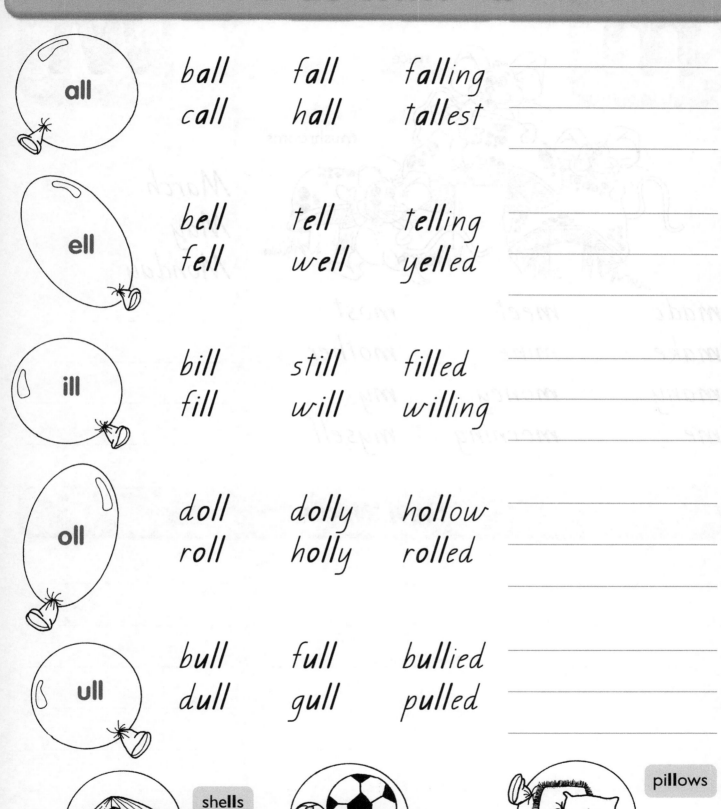

all

| ball | fall | falling |
| call | hall | tallest |

ell

| bell | tell | telling |
| fell | well | yelled |

ill

| bill | still | filled |
| fill | will | willing |

oll

| doll | dolly | hollow |
| roll | holly | rolled |

ull

| bull | full | bullied |
| dull | gull | pulled |

shells

balls

pillows

mice

mushrooms

March
May
Monday

made	meet	most
make	mine	mother
many	money	my
me	morning	myself

New Words

mm

The baby has a yu**mm**y du**mm**y.

comma _____

common _____

drummer _____

hammer _____

mammal _____

summer _____

Double the "m" before you add the new ending.

cram	dim	drum	hum
cramming	dimmed	drummed	hummed
ram	slam	swim	trim
ramming	slammed	swimmer	trimming

Me

thumb

eyebrow

eye

ear

wrist

cheek

teeth

mouth

tongue

shoulder

arm

chest

nose

forehead

waist

elbow

chin

hair

neck

hip

fingers

hand

leg

knee

toenail

ankle

foot

toes

heel

feet

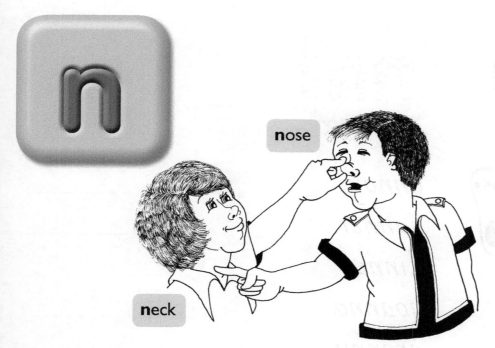

nose

neck

New South Wales Northern Territory November

name	never	night	
narrow	new	no	
near	next	nothing	
need	nice	now	

New Words

annoy
banner
dinner
goanna
granny
nanny

_____

_____

_____

_____

_____

_____

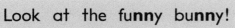
Look at the funn**y bu**nn**y!**

Double the "n" before you add the new ending.

fan	grin	pin	plan
fanned	grinned	pinning	planning
stun	sun	thin	win
stunned	sunny	thinner	winning

Words Ending in "ng"

sing

bring
fling
ring
sting

_____
_____
_____
_____

sang

bang
gang
hang
rang

_____
_____
_____
_____

song

gong
long
strong
wrong

_____
_____
_____
_____

sung

flung
hung
lung
rung

_____
_____
_____
_____

Numbers

1	one	first		2	two	second
3	three	third		4	four	fourth
5	five	fifth		6	six	sixth
7	seven	seventh		8	eight	eighth
9	nine	ninth		10	ten	tenth

11	eleven	eleventh		12	twelve	twelfth
13	thirteen	thirteenth		14	fourteen	fourteenth
15	fifteen	fifteenth		16	sixteen	sixteenth
17	seventeen	seventeenth		18	eighteen	eighteenth
19	nineteen	nineteenth		20	twenty	twentieth

oranges

octopus

October
Olympics
Owen

oblong   old   other
o'clock   only   our
of   open   out
off   or   over

New Words

Rhyming Words for

bog
blog
fog
log

I love my **dog**.

_____

_____

_____

_____

drop
flop
mop
stop

I can **hop**.

_____

_____

_____

_____

got
lot
not
pot

Take a ride in a **hot** air balloon.

_____

_____

_____

_____

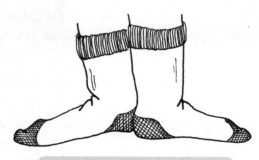

block
clock
flock
rock

My **socks** are warm.

_____

_____

_____

_____

p P

pelican

parrot

Pacific Ocean
Perth
Phan

paint	pillow	pretty
party	play	pull
pass	please	put
past	pool	pyjamas

New Words

pp

Pepper makes me sneeze!

a-a-a-choo...

apple
floppy
happy
nappy
puppy
slippers

Double the "p" before you add the new ending.

chop	clap	drop	hop
chopped	clapped	dropping	hopped
mop	shop	skip	whip
mopping	shopping	skipping	whipped

Pets

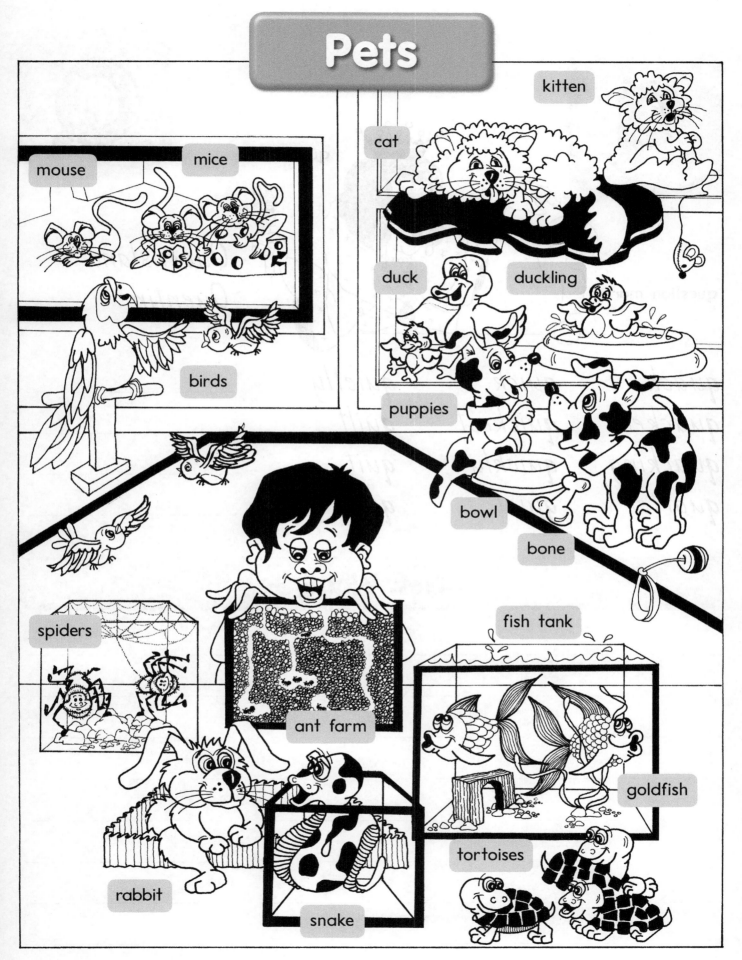

kitten

cat

mouse

mice

duck

duckling

birds

puppies

bowl

bone

spiders

fish tank

ant farm

goldfish

tortoises

rabbit

snake

q   Q

queen

question mark

Queensland
Quentin

quack   quick   quietly   _____
quacked   quickest   quilt   _____
quacking   quickly   quit   _____
quarter   quiet   quite   _____

New Words

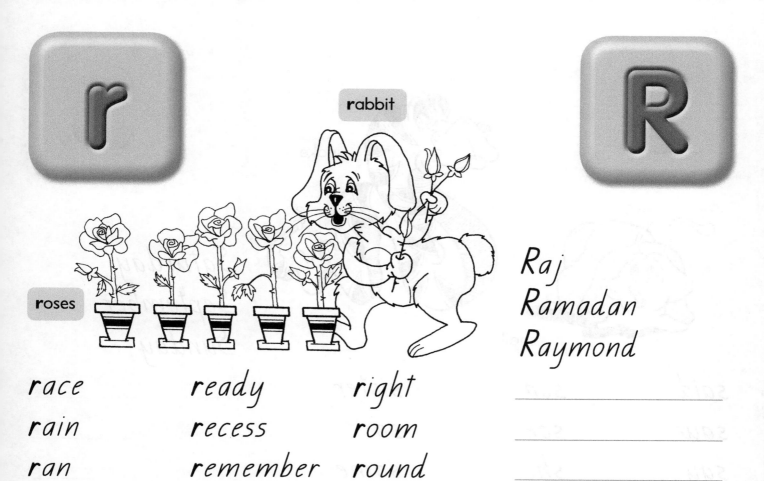

r   rabbit   **R**

roses

Raj
Ramadan
Raymond

race	ready	right
rain	recess	room
ran	remember	round
read	ride	ruler

_____
_____
_____
_____

New Words

snake

snail

Saturday
September
Sunday

said	*sea*	*sister*
saw	*see*	*so*
say	*she*	*some*
school	*sick*	*someone*

New Words

Adding "s"

dog	duck	egg	lick	thing
dogs	ducks	eggs	licks	things

Adding "es"

box	bus	catch	miss	pinch
boxes	buses	catches	misses	pinches

School Classroom

activities
alphabet
art

bookcase
books
brushes

calculator
chairs
charts
computer
craft

desks
drama
draw

drawing-pin
drawings

English
experiments

games
glue

handwriting
history

interactive
  whiteboard

maps
maths

paint
paintings
paper
pencil case
pencil sharpener
pens
printer
puzzles

read
rewards
ruler

science
scissors
stapler
sticky tape

stories
string
sums

table
teacher
television
tests
timetable
toys
trophies

whiteboard
whiteboard
  markers
words
write

School Playground

asphalt

balls
basketballs
benches
bubblers

canteen
children
classrooms
climbing frame

fence
flagpole
flowers
footballs

gardens
goalposts

hats
hopscotch
hula hoops

loudspeaker
lunch box

office
oval

playing area
principal

recycling bin
rubbish bin

sandpit
seats
shelter
skipping ropes
steps
sunscreen
swings

teacher
toilet
trees

When "s" and "h" stand next to each other ...

shark

sh is their new sound.

shack	sheep	shock
shade	sheet	shop
she	shin	shot
shed	shine	shut

fish

ash	hush	_____
bash	rash	_____
dash	rush	_____
		_____

Shapes

circle   hexagon   pentagon   square

diamond   oval   rectangle   triangle

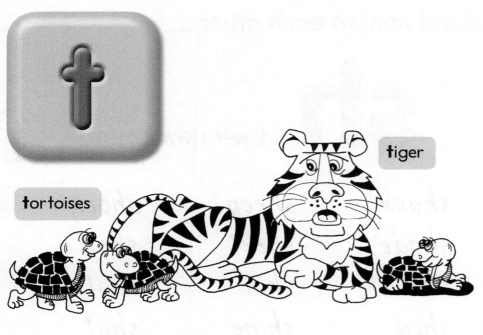

tortoises

tiger

Tasmania
Thursday
Tuesday

take	today	tree
teacher	tomorrow	tried
the	too	truck
to	took	try

New Words

54

better
butter
flutter
gutter
matter
pretty

I'm little!

Double the "t" before you add the new ending.

bat	chat	cut	let
batted	chatted	cutting	letting
pat	shut	spot	trot
patted	shutting	spotted	trotting

Technology

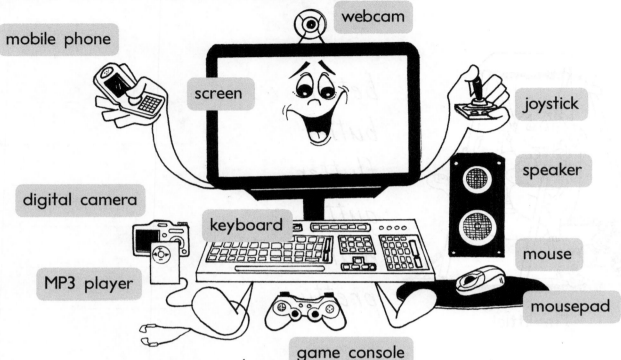

mobile phone · webcam · screen · joystick · speaker · digital camera · keyboard · mouse · MP3 player · mousepad · game console

blog
byte
chat
computer
connect
disk
download
email
game
headphones
icon
Internet

joystick
password
photograph
pixel
ringtone
scan
search
television
text
touch screen
virus
volume

Connect to the Internet.
Delete junk mail.
Download a file.
Exit a program.
Insert a disk.
Listen to music on your
    MP3 player.
Play a computer game.
Scan a picture.
Search the World Wide Web.
Send an email.
Shut down the computer.
Text message a friend.
Upload a photo.

When "t" and "h" stand next to each other ...

 **is their new sound.**

throw

than	then
that	there
their	these
them	this

_____

_____

_____

_____

thank	thing
thick	think
thief	thrill
thin	thumb

_____

_____

_____

_____

fourth

bother	bath
brother	both
father	broth
feather	cloth
mother	fifth
other	growth
slither	moth

_____

_____

_____

_____

_____

_____

_____

Time

yesterday today tomorrow	morning recess lunchtime night	second minute hour	spring summer autumn winter
calendar day week weekend fortnight month year	clock watch half past o'clock quarter past quarter to		early before after later soon

Important Dates to Remember

Event	Date
My birthday	

58

U

umbrellas   **u**p

Uluru
Umiko
United States

ugly	*unhappy*	*upset*
uncle	*unless*	*us*
under	*until*	*use*
undo	*upon*	*useful*

New Words

Rhyming Words for

bug
hug
rug
tug

fun
run
stun
sun

This is my **mug**.

Would you like a
hot cross **bun**?

_____

_____

_____

_____

_____

_____

but
cut
nut
shut

buck
luck
suck
tuck

I live in a grass **hut**.

I see a wet **duck**!

_____

_____

_____

_____

_____

_____

V

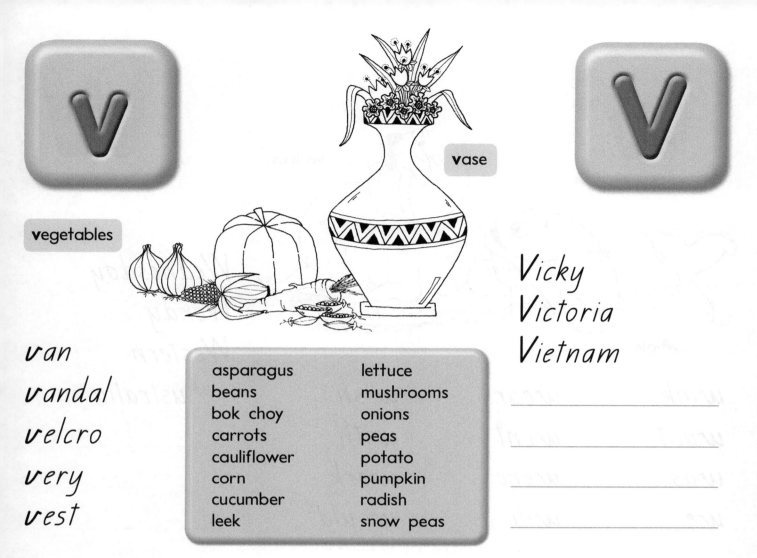

vegetables

vase

*v*an
*v*andal
*v*elcro
*v*ery
*v*est

asparagus	lettuce
beans	mushrooms
bok choy	onions
carrots	peas
cauliflower	potato
corn	pumpkin
cucumber	radish
leek	snow peas

Vicky
Victoria
Vietnam

New Words

walrus

whale

Wednesday
Wendy
Western
Australia

walk	*wear*	*wish*
want	*went*	*with*
was	*were*	*work*
we	*will*	*would*

New Words

When "w" and "h" stand next to each other ...

wh is their new sound.

wheels

what
when
which
why

who
whole
whose

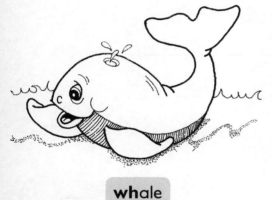

whale

wheel
whip
white
whiz

_____
_____
_____
_____

whistle

anywhere
nowhere
whenever
whimper
whistle

_____
_____
_____
_____
_____

X

fox

box

mix

ox

six

X-ray

xylophone

Y

yoyo

yacht

yard

year

yell

yellow

yesterday

Z

zebra

breeze

sneeze

wheeze

zero

zip

zoo